All Woman Soul

Production: Sadie Cook
Published 1998

© International Music Publications Limited
Southend Road, Woodford Green, Essex IG8 8HN, England
Reproducing this music in any form is illegal and forbidden by the Copyright, Designs and Patents Act 1988

B-A-B-Y

Words and Music by
ISAAC HAYES and
DAVID PORTER

4

Verse 3:   (I said) ba-by, oh baby, you look so good to me baby
Baby, oh baby, I love for you to call me baby.
When you squeeze me real tight, you know you make the
Wrong things right, and I can't stop loving you,
And I won't stop calling you

To Chorus *(Repeat & ad: lib vocals to FADE)*

CAR WASH

Words and Music by
NORMAN WHITFIELD

6

CHAIN OF FOOLS

Words and Music by
DONALD COVAY

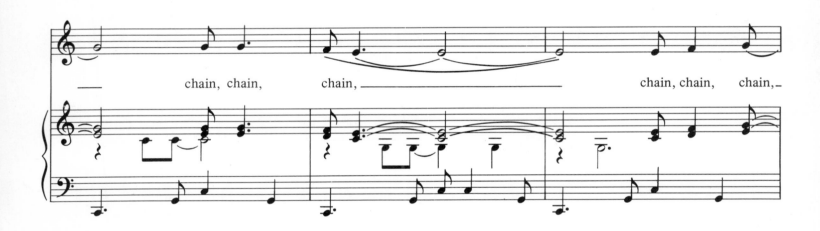

For five long years ___ I thought you ___ were my man, ___ But I found out, love, ___ I'm just a link in your chain. ___ You got me where you want me I ain't no-thin' but your fool. _____

DANCING IN THE STREET

Words and Music by
MARVIN GAYE, IVY JO HUNTER
and WILLIAM STEVENSON

I FEEL FOR YOU

Words and Music by
PRINCE

Moderately bright

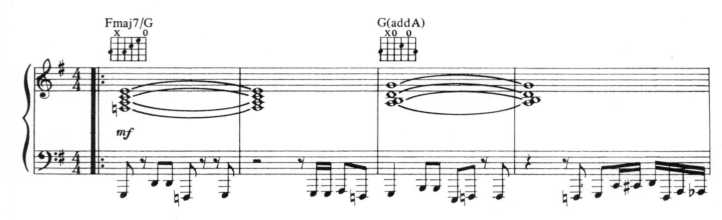

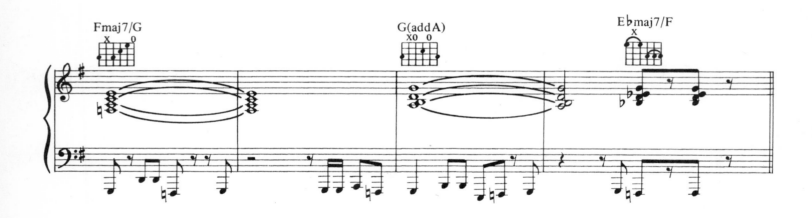

Ba - by, ba - by, when I look at you, I get a warm feel - ing in - side.

Ba - by, ba - by, when I lay with you, there's no place I'd rath - er be.

I PUT A SPELL ON YOU

Words and Music by
JAY HAWKINS

DON'T LET GO (LOVE)

Words and Music by
IVAN MATIAS, ANDREA MARTIN,
MARQUEZE ETHERIDGE
and ORGANIZED NOIZE

JIMMY MACK

Words and Music by
BRIAN HOLLAND, LAMONT DOZIER
and EDDIE HOLLAND

Moderately steady 4 shuffle

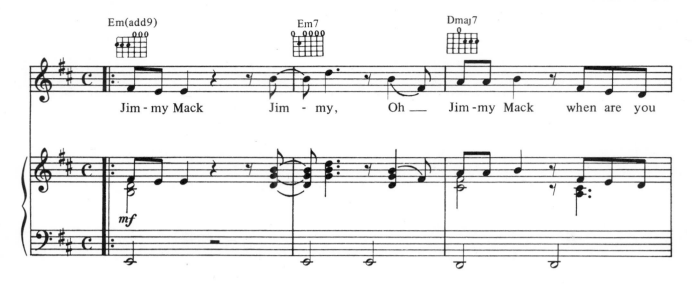

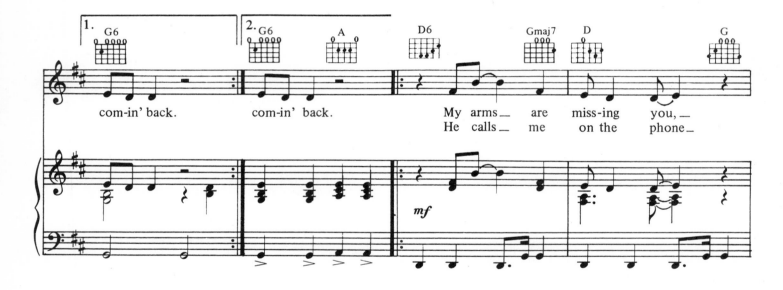

IT SHOULD HAVE BEEN ME

Words and Music by
NORMAN WHITFIELD
and WILLIAM STEVENSON

I saw my love walk - ing down the

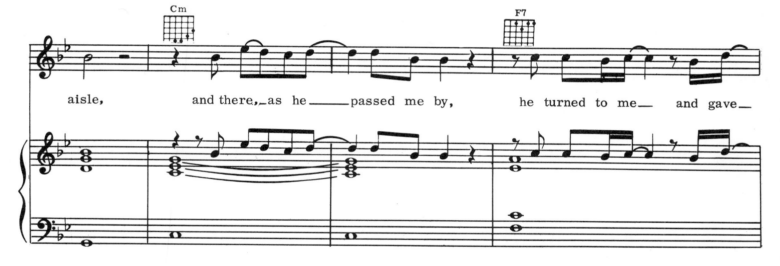

aisle, and there, as he passed me by, he turned to me and gave

me a smile.
Then the preach - er, then the preach - er,
Then the preach - er, oh yeah,

LADY MARMALADE

Words and Music by
BOB CREWE and KENNY NOLAN

Hey, sis-ter, go sis-ter, soul sis-ter, go sis-ter, met Mar-ma-lade down in ol'

New Or-leans, strut-tin' her stuff on the street. She say,

"Hel-lo, hey Joe, ya wan-na give it a go?" 'N get chor get chor ya da da.

Get chor get chor ya ya he ya. Mo-cha cho-co-la-ta ya

MIDNIGHT TRAIN TO GEORGIA

Words and Music by
JIM WEATHERLY

1. L. A. proved too much for the man,
2. He kept dream-in' that some day he'd be a star,

so he's leav - in' the life he's
but he sure found out the hard way that dreams don't

come to know.
al - ways come true.

He said he's go - in' back to find,
So, he pawned all his hopes,

4

said he's go-in' back to a sim-pler place and time. _____

_____ And I'll be with him on that mid-night train to Geor-gia;

I'd rath-er live in his world ___ than live with-out him in mine.

Go, gon-na board, gon-na board gon-na board, the mid-night train; got-ta

REACH OUT, I'LL BE THERE

Words and Music by
BRIAN HOLLAND, LAMONT DOZIER
and EDDIE HOLLAND

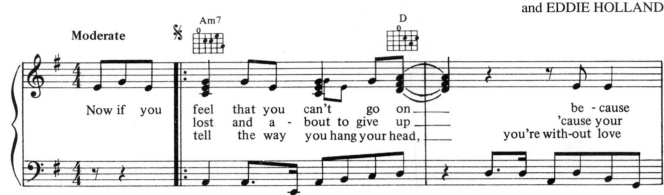

Now if you feel that you can't go on _____ be - cause
lost and a - bout to give up _____ 'cause your
tell the way you hang your head, _____ you're with-out love

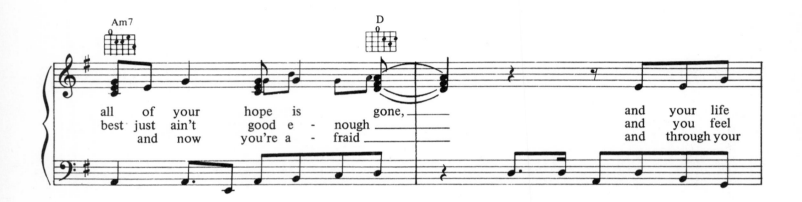

all of your hope is gone, _____ and your life
best just ain't good e - nough, _____ and you feel
and now you're a - fraid _____ and through your

is filled with much con-fu - sion _____ un-til
the world has grown cold, _____ and you're
tears you look a-round, _____ but there's no

hap-pi - ness _____ is just an il - lu -
drift-ing out _____ all on your own,
peace of mind _____ to be found,

_____ sion, and your world _____ a - round _____ is crum - blin' down; _____
_____ and you need _____ a hand to hold; _____
(Spoken) I know what you're thinkin', you're alone now, no love of

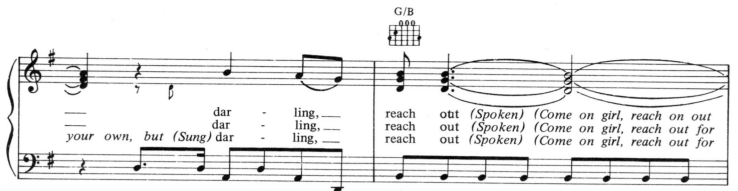

dar - ling, ___ reach out (Spoken) (Come on girl, reach on out
dar - ling, ___ reach out (Spoken) (Come on girl, reach out for
your own, but (Sung) dar - ling, ___ reach out (Spoken) (Come on girl, reach out for

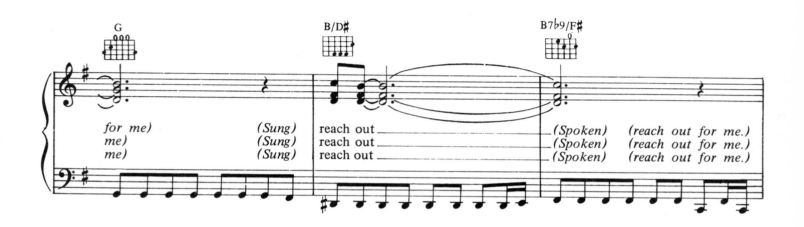

for me) (Sung) reach out _____ (Spoken) (reach out for me.)
me) (Sung) reach out _____ (Spoken) (reach out for me.)
me) (Sung) reach out _____ (Spoken) (reach out for me.)

(Sung) I'll be there, ___ with a
I'll be there, ___ to
Just look over your shoulder, I'll be there, ___ to

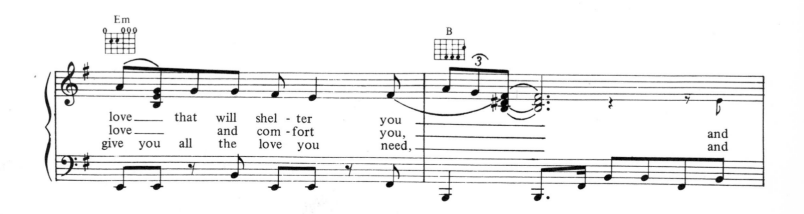

love ___ that will shel - ter you ___
love ___ and com - fort you ___ and
give you all the love you need, ___ and

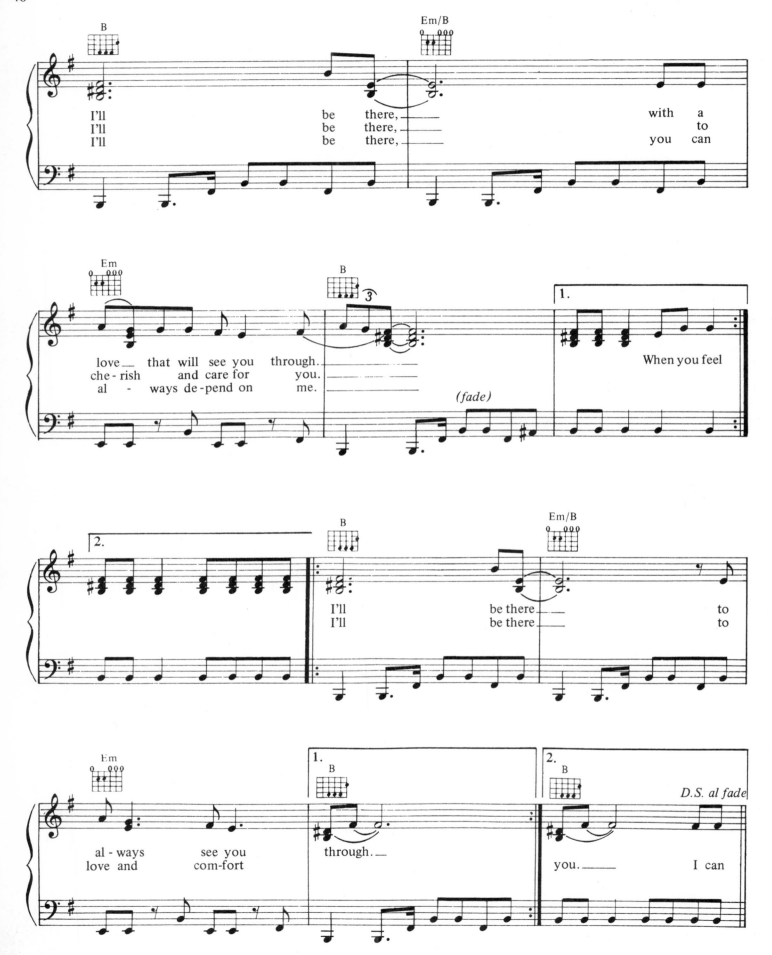

RIVER DEEP MOUNTAIN HIGH

Words and Music by
PHIL SPECTOR, ELLIE GREENWICH
and JEFF BARRY

When I was a lit-tle girl ____ I had a rag ____ doll,
you have a pup-py ____

The on-ly doll ____ I've ev-er owned. ____
That al-ways fol - lowed you a - round? ____

-er,— let me say,— And it gets high-
-ger, ba - by, and hea-ven knows, — And it gets sweet-

-er— day by day.—
-er, ba - by, as it grows._

Chorus

Do I love you, right or wrong?_____ Yeah

riv - er   deep,   moun-tain high, ___   yeah   yeah yeah. ___

If   I   lost you,   would I   cry? ___

I   would,   ba - by, ___   ba - by, ___   ba - by. ___

fine

When you were a young boy did ___

a tempo

SPANISH HARLEM

Words and Music by
JERRY LEIBER
and PHIL SPECTOR

STOP! IN THE NAME OF LOVE

Words and Music by
BRIAN HOLLAND, LAMONT DOZIER
and EDDIE HOLLAND

UNTIL YOU COME BACK TO ME
(THAT'S WHAT I'M GONNA DO)

Words and Music by
STEVIE WONDER, MORRIS BROADNAX
and CLARENCE PAUL

VERSE 2:
Why did you have to decide
You had to set me free?
I'm going to swallow my pride, (my pride)
And beg you to please see me.
(Baby won't you see me?)
I'm going to walk by myself
Just to prove that my love is true;
All for you baby.
(*To Chorus:*)

VERSE 3:
Although your phone you ignore,
Somehow I must, somehow I must,
How I must explain.
I'm gonna rap on your door,
Tap on your window pane.
(Tap on your window pane.)
I'm gonna camp on your steps
Until I get through to you;
I've got to change your view, baby.
(*To Chorus:*)

WE ARE FAMILY

Words and Music by
BERNARD EDWARDS
and NILE ROGERS

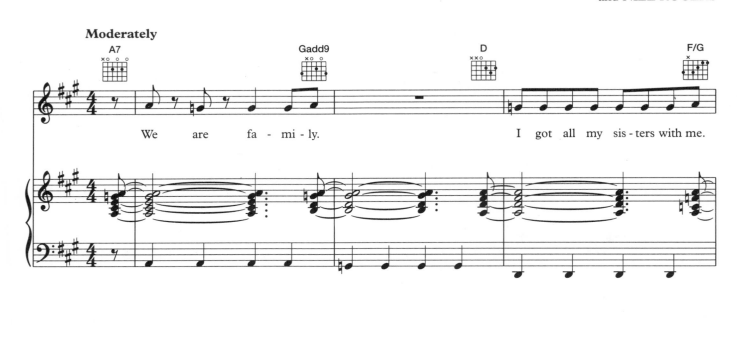

We are fa - mi - ly. I got all my sis - ters with me.

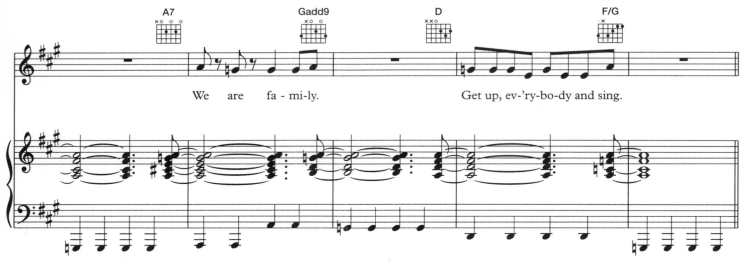

We are fa - mi - ly. Get up, ev-'ry-bo-dy and sing.

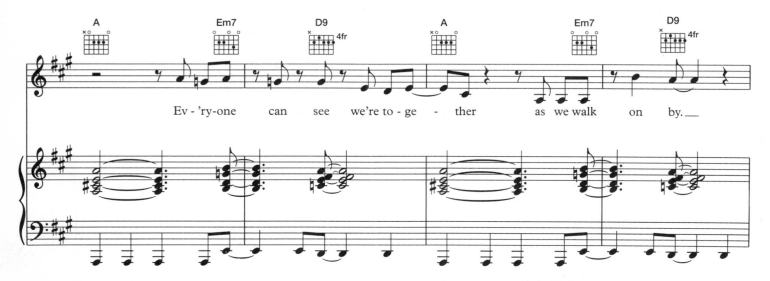

Ev - 'ry-one can see we're to - ge - ther as we walk on by. ___

WHERE DO BROKEN HEARTS GO?

Words and Music by
FRANK WILDHORN
and CHUCK JACKSON

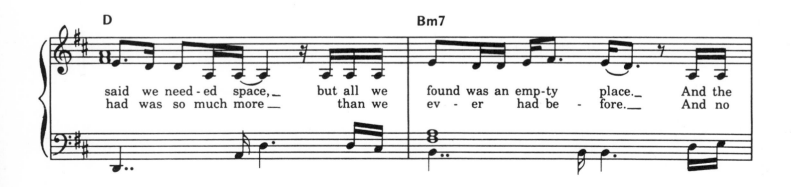

on - ly things I learned   is that I   need you des -   p'rate - ly.
mat - ter now I try,   you're   al - ways on   my mind.
So

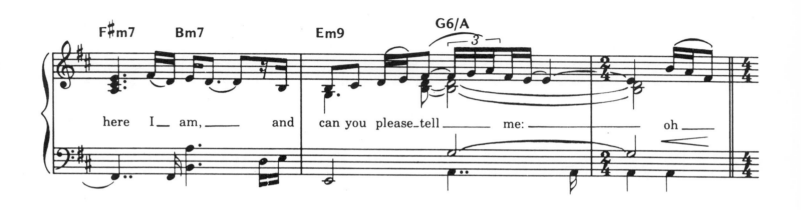

here I   am,   and   can you please tell   me: oh

Chorus:

Where do bro-ken hearts go;   can they find their   way home   back to the o - pen arms of a

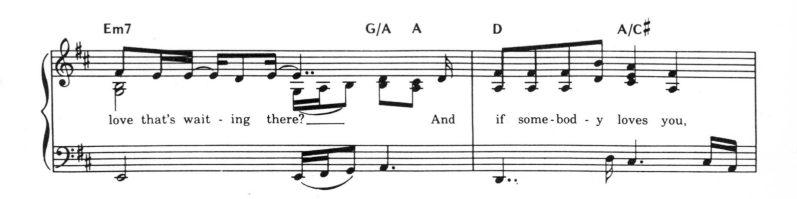

love that's wait - ing there?   And   if some-bod - y loves you,

won't they al - ways ___ love ___ you? I look in your eyes, ___ and I

1. know that you _ still care ___ for **2.** know that you _ still care ___ for me. ___ And

Bridge:

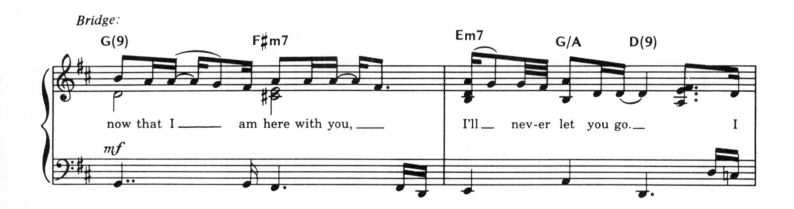

now that I _____ am here with you, ___ I'll ___ nev-er let you go. ___ I

look in-to _ your _ eyes, _ and now _ I know, now I know.

WOMAN

Words and Music by
NENEH CHERRY, CAMERON McVEY
and JOHNNY DOLLAR

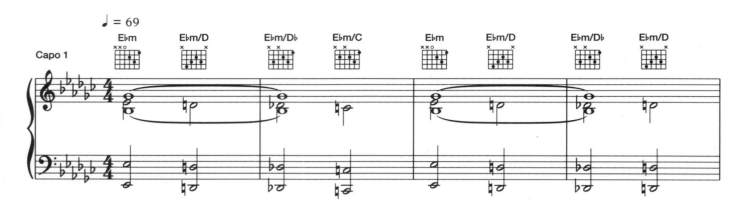

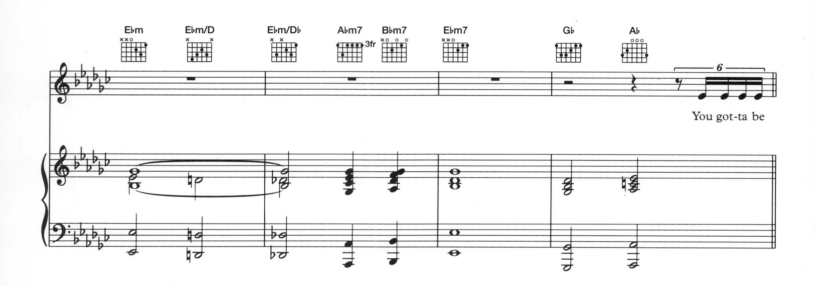

You got-ta be

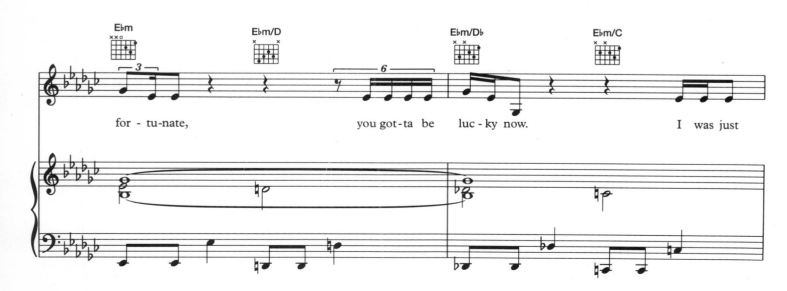

for - tu-nate,   you got-ta be luc - ky now.   I was just

TELL ME SOMETHING GOOD

Words and Music by
STEVIE WONDER

YOU CAN'T HURRY LOVE

Words and Music by
BRIAN HOLLAND, EDDIE HOLLAND
and LAMONT DOZIER

YOUR LOVE IS KING

Words and Music by
ADU and MATTHEWMAN

king _____ crown you with my heart, __ your love is king, _____ {(1,3,)
(2) You're the

YOU'RE ALL I NEED TO GET BY

Words and Music by
NICKOLAS ASHFORD
and VALERIE SIMPSON

2. Like an eagle protects his nest, for you I'll do my best.
   Stand by you like a tree, and dare anybody to try and move me.
   Darling in you I found strength where I was torn down.
   Don't know what's in store, but together we can open any door.

3. Just to do what's good for you, and inspire you a little higher.
   I know you can make a man out of a soul that did'nt have a goal
   'Cause we, we got the right foundation, and with love and
   Determination, you're all, you're all I want to strive for;
   And do a little more all, all the joys under the sun,
   Wrapped up into one, you're all, you're all I need,
   You're all I need, You're all I need To get by
   All I need to get by.

STONED LOVE

Words and Music by
YENNIK SAMOHT
and FRANK WILSON

The Woman Series
All ... Series

All Woman
volume one

Contents include: All Woman; Do You Know Where You're Going To?; Ev'ry Time We Say Goodbye;
Fever; I Am What I Am; I Will Always Love You; Miss You Like Crazy; Summertime;
Superwoman; What's Love Got To Do With It and Why Do Fools Fall In Love.
Order Ref: 19076

All Woman
volume two

Contents include: Don't It Make My Brown Eyes Blue; Giving You The Best That I Got;
Killing Me Softly With His Song; Memory; One Moment In Time; Pearl's A Singer;
That Ole Devil Called Love; Walk On By; The Wind Beneath My Wings and You Don't Have To Say You Love Me.
Order Ref: 2043A

All Woman
volume three

Contents include: Almaz; Big Spender; Crazy For You; Fame; The First Time Ever I Saw Your Face;
From A Distance; Love Letters; My Baby Just Cares For Me; My Funny Valentine; The Power Of Love;
Promise Me; Saving All My Love For You and Total Eclipse Of The Heart.
Order Ref: 2444A

All Woman
volume four

Contents include: Anything For You; Evergreen; For Your Eyes Only; I Will Survive; Mad About The Boy;
A Rainy Night in Georgia; Send In The Clowns; Smooth Operator; Sophisticated Lady; Stay With Me Till Dawn;
Sweet Love; Think Twice and Touch Me In The Morning.
Order Ref: 3034A

All Woman
Blues

Contents include: Body and Soul; Georgia On My Mind; God Bless' The Child;
I Don't Stand A Ghost Of A Chance With You; I Gotta Right To Sing The Blues; I'd Rather Go Blind;
Lover Man (Oh, Where Can You Be?); Mood Indigo; Stormy Weather and You've Changed.
Order Ref: 3690A

All Woman
Cabaret

Contents include: Almost Like Being In Love; Another Openin', Another Show; Anything Goes;
For Once In My Life; Goldfinger; I Won't Last A Day Without You; If My Friends Could See Me Now;
My Way; New York New York; People and There's No Business Like Show Business.
Order Ref: 3691A

All Woman
Jazz

Contents include: Bewitched; Crazy He Calls Me; A Foggy Day; Girl From Ipanema; How High The Moon;
I'm In The Mood For Love; It Don't Mean A Thing (If It Ain't Got That Swing); It's Only A Paper Moon;
Misty; On Green Dolphin Street; 'Round Midnight and Straighten Up And Fly Right.
Order Ref: 4778A